more sweetness will unfold tomorrow…

—l.l. barkat

Beyond the Glass

poems

l.l. barkat

𝑡𝑠 T. S. Poetry Press • New York

T. S. Poetry Press
New York
Tspoetry.com

© 2025 by L.L. Barkat
All rights reserved.

Cover image by Maria Louceiro. Unsplash+ license.
https://unsplash.com/@marialouceiro

ISBN 978-1-943120-78-9

Barkat, L.L.
    [Poetry.]
    Beyond the Glass: Poems
    ISBN 978-1-943120-78-9

*for bethany,
who never stopped believing*

CONTENTS

Prelude 13
A Bonus Poem Before We Begin 15
Sparrow Beyond the Glass 15
The 30 Poems 17
1-sparrow 19
2-would 20
3-Night 21
4-Writing to the "Favorite Hot Drink" Prompt............22
5-After a Collage by Catherine Abbey Hodges 24
6-First Memory, Cherished 26
7-Despereaux, Darling 27
8-Salary 28
9-The Big Red Heart Box 30
10-Ford Torino 31
11-Father Fashion 32
12-Titania's Note Left by the Door,
     Photocopied by Oberon 34
13-Giveaway 36
14-Plaint 38
15-After Emily 39
16-Cut 40
17-1930s Bedroom Closet 41
18-Grand Jury 42
19-Secrets (Yours) 43
20-Sloansville II 44

21-To the Road That Intersects Corbin Hill,
   Where a Corner Store Sold Orange Creamsicles
   (Which I Loved) 45
22-Avatar 47
23-Lessons in Glass 49
24-Photograph: Aruba, 1938 50
25-Twins with My Sister's Steel Grey 52
26-Repair Woman 54
27-Paris to London, 1992 55
28-To Earth 57
29-Garnet 58
30-The Spice Carousel 59
The 30 Prompts 60

PRELUDE

This year, for National Poetry Month, *The Write to Poetry* offered a 30-Day Challenge—thirty prompts to take us back and send us forward.

I decided to write to **all thirty**, regardless of how inspired I felt regarding any given prompt. (If you'd like to try the challenge yourself, you can find all thirty prompts at the end of this collection.)

Ordinarily, I'm not the kind of poet who writes to prompts. My poems tend to come from real-time experience, through the sudden, colliding juxtaposition of an image and an emotion, as if they were meant to be together. How could I refuse to give them partnership in a poem?

Yet, for the past seven years, I had fewer and fewer of these poem-writing experiences. In fact, I developed a very sound case of writer's block. This was startling! I've always been an extraordinarily prolific writer. Then, the writing evaporated. What an empty landscape it has been.

There are logical reasons for this, I am sure. Things to do with cognitive and emotional overload, coupled with not enough time to simply unwind. Distractions, too, and a sense of not knowing when a host of challenges would end (if ever).

It was in this discouraging context that I decided to try something entirely (for me) new: to write to prompts for an extended period. I would push myself to pen poems even when I felt nothing—or, worse, when I felt exhausted and disinterested.

What resulted is a collection that has a certain voice and vision. A kind of looking forward and looking back, just as the prompts promised to give us. I hope you enjoy these hard-won poems. They are my gift to you for moments when you think you cannot go on. You can. Against all odds, you can.

A BONUS POEM BEFORE WE BEGIN

For the very first prompt of the 30-Day Challenge, I also wrote a ghazal. The style is rather different from the rest of the poems in this collection, and the themes feel aptly placed beforehand, so I prefer to share it with you here as a bonus…

Sparrow Beyond the Glass

There you are, all wings and flitting—unthinking of your untold tomorrow;
You play amidst cherry blossoms, unworried; more sweetness will unfold tomorrow.

How lightly you take flight, leave the blossoms touched with a blue-bold sky;
Tiny buds wait for your wings to return at sunset, the gold of tomorrow.

There are some who would like your home to be sold for a song;
But where would you play, then, as the earth unrolled tomorrow?

The drum of morning beats 'til the hour is annulled;
Perhaps you will bring back a mate to remold tomorrow.

Inside, I stand by the glass, shake into a cherry sweater, now old
Ask you, as if you could know: will it still be this cold tomorrow?

THE 30 POEMS

1

sparrow

in the cherry blossoms
how free
how joyous

the glass
between us—
how thin
a barrier.

2

would

that you'd
give me
a white lily

all memory
no desire

its whole face true
its dark pollen
without stain

across
what's past

beyond
what's lost

3

Night

falls
above
the Hudson

Venus
letting down
her hair
into the
early stars

Moon rises
over
the mountains

4

Writing to the "Favorite Hot Drink" Prompt

I wish it was as simple as saying,
"I love tea," then my poem
could be done and I could be free

to move on to my morning's next business
which is almonds and berries, whichever
I can procure (not the almonds, which are

always tamari)—

raspberry, blackberry, blueberry

Grandmother, you spoiled me
and these store-boughts serve to remind
of your endless love, how you planted
mulberry, gooseberry, strawberry,
currant berry (*raspberry, blackberry blueberry*).

So, I splurge!

But back to the tea, for which
explanations steep in complexity.

Mother was Lipton,
but life has revealed to me
an evergreen with many iterations

and I am lost
trying to land
on a favorite

please don't make me

This morning it's black
(a French "Noelle").

Yesterday, a Chinese green
from a gift box given long ago
by my daring sister
(instant addiction, but alas,
I don't know your name,
hand-sewn leaves with—
what's that, a chrysanthemum
flowering at your center?)

If I catalog every oolong,
jasmine, sencha, phoenix,
long jing, assam,
we'll be here all day.

Suffice it to say,
I love (*adore!*)

my morning tea.

5

After a Collage by Catherine Abbey Hodges

If a poem
is a hope galaxy
(as Catherine's art
suggests to me)

I'm all for
traveling
the stars

each line a jewel
in Orion's
ancient belt

each thought
a dip
into the
Milky Way

of what has
been lost
somehow turning

into what has
been found
star-dusted

at the edge
of what we
thought we knew

when the lines
set out

Light comes
at the fringe
of the comet's
tail

where the poem
begins

where it turns
(and turns again)
the constellation

of your
heart.

6

First Memory, Cherished

White tiles
Daddy smiling
in the gentle
rain

7

Despereaux, Darling,

how they ridiculed you
for believing
in love, in *story,*

and you went
to the dungeon
for all that enamored

Did they understand
that the red thread
they meant as your
undoing

would become
a circlet

I'd never
want
to forget?

8

Salary

My daughter
smiles at me
sleepy-headed,
braid undone
from the night

I've been
reading
all about jobs
I might need

to take
to survive

Her aliveness
unfurls
by the glass

(outside, spring flowers
are coming into their own)

and the moment
catches

How do they
calculate
such pay?

A day spent
collecting
jasmine tea
her smile at me
cherry blossoms
scent of pine
sure rain

9

The Big Red Heart Box

holds chocolates
I can't wait to taste, so

I take a bite of too many

But then, who makes
the rules here, anyway?
A poem is a chocolate
(That's my rule)

Each page in a collection—
is an invitation

to taste as many as I like
in a single night

That strawberry
that caramel
that dark art

It doesn't matter
where I end

(Or where
I start)

10

Ford Torino

White boat, road drifter
steering barely

hinged to your chassis

How free I felt
making my way

down the road
in a seat that never

ended

Windows hand-levered
to let in the sun

or keep out
the rain

$500 flat—

my first freedom train

11

Father Fashion

It occurs to me
that I cannot remember
a thing you've worn.

Do you even own jeans?

You must.

And I remember
one of your wives
complaining of flannel.

But, for the life of me,
I cannot recall

a single thing
you've spent
the day in.

It must be your eyes
and your smile

and the way
something is always
BIG on your mind.

I admit that I
never took time
to consider your
fashion—

only your
laugh
and your
passion for
words.

12

**Titania's Note Left by the Door,
Photocopied by Oberon**

It's not
that I don't
love you
still

I do

But there
are things
in life
that can't be

retracted

rivers, as you
once told me,
that can't be

stepped into
twice—
for if way leads
to way

in the woods,

how much
more does
water flow
off to the sea

without you
and me?

13

Giveaway

I didn't discard it
exactly.

There was a man.

He sat strategically
in front of the Courthouse.

Brides would descend,
newly justice-married,
roses or lilies in hand.

He had a camera.

Photos of happy couples
were pinned to a board.

He was an artist,

making his clever way
while the city pigeons
looked on.

I knew right then
he needed to have
what I wanted
to give away.

He was so happy.

Kept saying,
"I love my new bag!"

It matched his pants,
he said—as if to suggest
the exchange had been
pre-ordained.

14

Plaint

All the woods
are filled with berries.

Grandmother's garden
was filled with berries.

The store shelves:
they haven't enough!

Still.

Who wants to take
their fill of berries?

I do.

With you.

15

After Emily

She found diamonds
in morning dew,

knew emeralds
from afternoons
of walking Amherst's
small wilds.

I think of her
tonight, as the golden
hour returns

pouring its light
on spring violets—

amethyst treasure
newly come,
just above the
hill of juniper.

16

Cut

All the beautiful

all the feathered hair,
Farrah-style

Madewell jeans
floral blouses.

None of it
was reachable

except,
I thought (wrongly),
by scissor so I

cut.

Mostly a disaster,
the chin-length
strips at least

curled beneath my chin—

a kind of stubborn
auburn-delicate
holding up.

17

1930s Bedroom Closet

Too small for me to fit in,
you dutifully hold

all I put of myself
(except myself).

No room for shoes,
barely room for clothes,

you ask what I really need,
and I am wishing

I knew
the answer.

18

Grand Jury

The red-haired attorney who brings us
so many cases I can't discuss,

involving so many things
I don't really want to consider

(even though I must),

explains, in jest, that her shoes
are here to entertain us.

I would love to wear those
black velvet heels

with the buckle at the ankle—
walk in her footwear

for a few years, or even just
one rainless morning.

19

Secrets (Yours)

There are things
I still hold

back,

ways I care
you wouldn't know.

I tell myself
it doesn't matter

(and maybe it doesn't).

But there is inside me
a sense that life—

while sometimes
shorter than we'd guess—

is often longer than we know.

So it matters,
to me.

A future that may
never come

but could.

20

Sloansville II

You've already got
one poem, which,
since you only have

one well-traveled street

ought to be
enough.

But there's
this prompt
to write to

and the question
of how many poems

it takes
to remember
the beginning

of my own

well-traveled
life.

21

**To the Road That Intersects Corbin Hill,
Where a Corner Store Sold Orange Creamsicles
(Which I Loved)**

You were dirt
and shale

all washing away

in spring
in winter
we could sleigh

right down
your middle

we were alone
in the hollow

did not know
the meaning
of your name

could never
have guessed
its relation

to a pointed tool
used to make holes
in the ground

where a hand
might plant

seeds
seedlings

in what others
might have mistaken

for only
stone

22

Avatar

I'm happy enough
being me—

have never even
cared to make

an avatar,

except that *one* gold ceiling
and the small brass zip,

which makes me wonder
if the real answer

to who I'd like to be
(if I had magic choices)

might find its heart
in some hidden

sapphire,
emerald,
ruby,

or elemental
metal

that quietly made its counsel
to anyone in need

of beauty—
or of art.

23

Lessons in Glass

Easy to see right through
you may live your whole life not knowing
you've only skimmed the surface

commonly used   melted down

the sand loses—

somewhere in between
coupled randomness

(a found poem based on https://www.corning.com/worldwide/en/
innovation/materials-science/glass/how-glass-made.html)

24

Photograph: Aruba, 1938

Beside
the wind-bent tree

a lone figure
in a beach-grass field

beautiful and strong
in your dark, stylish
hand-made
dress.

You gaze at a point
that feels beyond me.

I'm here, now,
in a place
you did not know

your love
would lead
me.

And I wait
for you

though you
are gone

and the day
is gone

and who knows
about the tree.

25

Twins with My Sister's Steel Grey

I call you
my Snow White
coat—

bought you
in Woodstock
right before

we went
to the candle
store.

You're the navy
to my sister's
steel grey.

She and I haven't been
dressed as twins
since the days

our seamstress
grandmother
treated us as such

(matching dresses, paired with purses!)

We aren't, of course. Twins,

except in our two
fairy tale coats

(and tenacious
hearts).

26

Repair Woman

I would like
to fix this poem,

but that would
assume

it already exists.

Of course,
if I keep typing

the lines will open
to my hand,

and then
I'll have a chance.

27

Paris to London, 1992

You were tall enough to see
what was being left behind,

but you trusted me
to remember
what I'd been carrying.

*(Note to self: never carry
more than you can fit squarely
in two hands.)*

We lost it
to some pilfering soul
who lifted the case
from the overhead compartment
as soon as we departed
from the train.

Brand new, high-end camera—
my gift to you—plus $250 cash.

Insurance replaced the losses,
so to speak.

Since then,
I've been trying to remember
what Parisian corner
sold the ice cream

and what graffiti
I stood before,
as you took my picture

and I made you laugh.

28

To Earth

O

in space
in time

before them
and after them

I whisper
into your skirt

a circle
of pain

to which you are
no stranger

You whisper
into my soul

space

and time

without them

only with you

29

Garnet

The color of the new leaves
of the peach tree, a surprise
from an origin, latent branch—

having been only emerald
before the hard,
hard winter.

The color of the scattered
treasure in our kitchen granite;
brightly set in stone.

A childhood ring which I loved,
long gone.

And the earrings
you brought me from a distant land,
glittering, shaped forever
like tear drops.

30

The Spice Carousel

Being a poet is like cinnamon,
warm and sweet—at least for me.

Occasional nutmeg, clove.

The punctuation of vanilla bean
just when you thought
nothing could bring you through.

It's what makes pumpkin
and apples into pie—

plain fruit, spice turned.

THE 30 PROMPTS

Here are the thirty prompts from *The Write to Poetry's* 30-Day Challenge. Maybe you'd like to try them. I'd love to read your poems, if you do.

1. Write a poem about a bird outside your window

2. Write a poem about a flower you wish someone would give you (or you wish you could give someone else)

3. Write a poem about morning or night—okay, sure, or afternoon

4. Write a poem about your favorite hot drink

5. Write a poem about writing poems

6. Write a poem about your first memory

7. Write a poem about a favorite book character

8. Write a poem about collecting something

9. Write a poem about reading poems

10. Write a poem about your first car (or a car you remember from childhood)

11. Write a poem about something you remember your mother or father wearing

12. Write a poem that speaks directly to someone you wish you could see again (or love again)

13. Write a poem about discarding something

14. Write a poem about berries

15. Write a poem about finding treasure

16. Write a poem about a haircut you regret

17. Write a poem about your closet

18. Write a poem about shoes you would wear if you were more daring (or more able)

19. Write a poem about a secret you carry

20. Write a poem about the town or city where you grew up

21. Write a poem to a road (use the road's name if it has a name)

22. Write a poem in which you become someone else you wish you could become

23. Write a poem about glass

24. Write a poem about an old photo

25. Write a poem about a coat you love (or really don't like)

26. Write a poem about fixing something

27. Write a poem about losing something

28. Write a poem to the Earth

29. Write a poem about a specific color

30. Write a poem about being a poet

ALSO FROM T. S. POETRY PRESS

Love, Etc.
by L.L. Barkat

www.ingramcontent.com/pod-product-compliance
Lightning Source LLC
Chambersburg PA
CBHW022109040426
42451CB00007B/193